good deed rain

Violet of the Silent Movies © 2020
Allen Frost, Good Deed Rain
Bellingham, Washington
ISBN: 9781647643874

Writing & Drawings: Allen Frost
Cover Image & Introduction Poster:
　courtesy of Josh Mersereau
Violet photos: Rustle Frost
Cover Production: Jen Armitage
Apple: TFK!

"It is music of my people far away. As long as you hear it, no harm will come to you. Do you recognize it?"

　—*I Love a Mystery* (1945)

VIOLET of the SILENT MOVIES

Allen Frost

39 Books by Allen Frost

...Ohio Trio...Bowl of Water...
....Another Life....Home Recordings....
...The Mermaid Translation...The Selected
Correspondence of Kenneth Patchen....
...The Wonderful Stupid Man...
..Saint Lemonade...Playground...Roosevelt..
....5 Novels....The Sylvan Moore Show....
...Town in a Cloud....A Flutter of Birds
Passing Through Heaven: A Tribute to Robert
Sund......At the Edge of America......
...Lake Erie Submarine....The Book of Ticks...
........I Can Only Imagine........
....The Orphanage of Abandoned Teenagers....
...Different Planet...Go with the Flow: A
Tribute to Clyde Sanborn...Homeless Sutra...
..The Lake Walker....A Hundred Dreams Ago..
....Almost Animals....The Robotic Age....
....Kennedy....Fable....Elbows & Knees:
Essays & Plays....The Last Paper Stars....
...Walt Amherst is Awake...When You Smile
You Let in Light....Pinocchio in America....
....Florida....Blue Anthem Wailing....
...The Welfare Office...Island Air...
....Imaginary Someone....
...Violet of the Silent Movies...

VIOLET of the SILENT MOVIES

Allen Frost

Good Deed Rain ◊ Bellingham, Washington ◊ 2020

INTRODUCTION

This book began with a visit to a local Hollywood memory collector. That's where we meet the featured star of this book, Violet Mersereau. Driving around this town full of houses, who would ever know behind the door in a cul-de-sac, her relative has turned a wall into her silent movie shrine. It makes you wonder what other family stories are hidden out there. Think of the museum they would make.

This summer I wrote to Charles Simic and asked him about something I read in a poetry interview. James Tate told him that Jesse James wrote haiku and letters to Rimbaud. Can that be true? Mr. Simic's response was, "He told me that in his family there was a rumor that they were related to the outlaw." That story also inspired this book and helped conjure all these characters.

This book follows in the footsteps of *Florida* and *The Welfare Office*. I've been enjoying writing poetry this way. *Elvis 42* is a very early collection of poems. Maybe my first, I forget. I made a hand-bound book of it and brought it to a bookstore in the University District. I hoped to sell them there. What was I thinking? I was like a green Jack London character! I never went back to see what happened, I guess the waves took care of them. And now, here we go again, as *Violet* joins that historic tide.

CONTENTS

Violet of the Silent Movies
The Fate of James Dean
The Creature Walks Among Us
The House on Haunted Hill
Champion the Wonder Horse
The Trampoline Apology
Job Security
The Witch in the Garage
Jack Spicer's Martian Radio
Just Like a Ghost
The Guitar of the Great Whackencracker
A Word
The Blackbird
13th & Failing
Buster Crabbe
Princess Condor
The Pied Piper Ice Cream Truck
Andrew the Birdhouse
Related to Roscoe
The Reunion
Places to Hide

A Taxi Song
The Second Time I Met Lee Van Cleef
A Factory on 32nd Street
Elvis 42
Turning to Water
Another Win for Seabiscuit
The Anti-Gravity Gravity Belt
Herman Snock Steals the Sun
The Buffalo Road
The Used Beluga
The Famous Last Words of a Dinosaur Trainer
Hedda Hopper
My New Folly
Movie Idea
A Hymn to Raking Leaves
Confessions of an Inventor
The Man Who Married a Dream
A Field in Oregon
Here in Mississippi
The Witch's House
15
Washed Ashore
Tribute to Red Skelton
Wearing a 1944 Movie
The Comedian

Something to Remember the Forest By
The Cattle Baron
Watching Esther Williams with my Daughter
Dante's Grill
Fay Wray Island
The Witch's Dog
The Magic Shop
Jesse James & Rimbaud
10 Feet off the Ground
Without Hamlet
The Wildlife on 32nd Street
Prince Charles
Lonzo
Watching the Whales
The Museum of Fluid Memory
The Dragonfly Junkyard
The Sweeper
The Caveman
It Helps to Know Someone
Haunting the House
Vincent Price and the Florist
In Defense of Mothra
The Five & Dime Robot
Under Your Spell
The Last Telegram

VIOLET of the SILENT MOVIES

I bet you never knew she is still there
on the hill in a house on Pacific View
pinned to the wall and glowing
like a butterfly chandelier
so that time holds her
quiet and unfading and
maybe more beautiful
than anything seen
in America today.

The FATE of JAMES DEAN

When they were young, he and his brother used Dean's poster as a dartboard. On a walk past their yard in 1955, you could hear their voices shrill and constant as long as the game continued.

The CREATURE WALKS AMONG US

Don wore the big heavy creature suit as he walked out of the surf and followed sidewalks. He was the sweetest person to know out by the trailer in the evening when the shoot was over, smoking cigarettes, telling stories and laughing, but his appearance in costume was enough to cause screams. Extras ran behind parked cars and sirens brought the police. The only reason he got out alive was because of the girl he carried. If he didn't have her, he wouldn't have anything. It was almost a love story. He let her go when he got to the shore. There wasn't much to say and anyway the bullets were flying. The water let him back underneath and the waves left no trace behind.

The HOUSE on HAUNTED HILL

They begged his mother to take them to the
Avalon. In 1959 they were barely ready for
the story up on the screen. They waited on
the curb afterwards, jumpy and checking the
street. They weren't afraid of Vincent Price,
they knew what they would have done. They
sat in the backseat and his mother listened
to them bray and when she couldn't take it
anymore, she turned the wheel and took them
the long way home through the cemetery.
With the headlights turned off, every shadow
was leaping at the sides of the car.

CHAMPION the WONDER HORSE

He's a famous movie star, why wouldn't I let him inside? I open the screen door and next thing I know he knocks over the coffee table and now he's eating the curtains off the window.

The TRAMPOLINE APOLOGY

Up and down and up and
down for years and
if it ever stops
there will be silence
time to be sorry
while searching the ground
looking for the words.

The right ones are
around here somewhere
waiting to be found
picked from the ruin
in the big dirt circle where
the grass once grew.

JOB SECURITY

A shovel is a temptation for Igor.
Left unattended by the corner of a garage
he can't resist taking hold, feeling
the smooth weight of it, imagining
the shriek of the soil.

The WITCH in the GARAGE

The garage door is open, a bonfire is going, a pile of brooms is burning in there. The jagged light from them spills out over the driveway and tumbles toward the sidewalk. I caught sight of her for only a moment until she saw she was being watched, then she snapped her fingers and went out like candlelight.

tumbles toward the sidewalk

the message is coming through

JACK SPICER'S MARTIAN RADIO

A basement apartment in North Beach is just as alive as Cape Canaveral. See it teeming with technicians in white shirts and ties, consoles and switches, and the smoke is heavy in the room. His hands are on the keys. The typewriter responds, the message is coming through, leaving a trail across the curling parchment.

JUST like a GHOST

The screen door
bangs shut
I feel the rattle
the tin cans fall
off the shelves
groceries roll
onto the floor

So it seems
every little thing in here
is tied by string to you
passing through

The GUITAR of the GREAT WHACKENCRACKER

What he was rests below
silver windows of the house
an old wooden place
renting rooms to the poor

Years of people
come and go
and after all the rain
wind and weather
time could deliver
onto the planted guitar of
The Great Whackencracker
it still grows in the garden
with the usual dandelions
tall green flavored weeds
lupines and stray colored other
cut down flowers

A WORD

The things you did
have been drawn
into a wind

The sound
echoes off walls
catches in trees
and carries on

The BLACKBIRD

I remember him
in a dark corner
in the backyard night
playing shadows
like a sailor
on a borrowed
guitar

Sometimes up higher
the lights on landing jets
blink like carried lanterns

Then
before I know it
it's close to dawn
the birds and The Beatles
singing "Here Comes The Sun"

13th & FAILING

I'll try to imagine
your new address

like a tidal pool
green as a garden
and calm too

Failing Street
a soft breeze

and 13th
the ripple

that carries
you home

BUSTER CRABBE

Fortunately our skies weren't always filled with rain. Sometimes business brought him our way. The TV screen showed him arriving in a sparking rocket ship. We always felt better knowing he was near, hovering over our city when we were kids.

PRINCESS CONDOR

After she left Hollywood, she bought a café in town on the side of the mountain. She wore plain clothes, no makeup, but she kept her name. Only the older patrons remembered her and they never gave her a hard time. She didn't want to make a fuss even though she could have cracked out of a condor egg.

The PIED PIPER ICE CREAM TRUCK

The song of it stings the hot air, floats like a fishing line finely cast across the neighborhood, between the houses, over lush green leaves and flowers, catching sunlight like a spider web. Look quick, the sound of children, screams and the patter of their little feet.

ANDREW the BIRDHOUSE

Once in shop class I made up a brother. Some nosy kid next to me kept asking me questions and my brother grew more and more. Before I knew it, he had a name and a car and a girlfriend. He even played electric guitar. I could barely keep up with the story. I was never so glad when it was my turn to use the band saw.

RELATED to ROSCOE

It's one of those things where you never know for sure. One of his relatives was married to Roscoe Arbuckle, the silent movie star. Maybe it's true, maybe it's not. It depends on who you talk to.

The REUNION

I dreamed I was sent back to school but none of the people I wanted to see were there. They had all grown and gone on to other lives of course, jobs and families and other cities far away. Some of them died. There really wasn't anything for me to do there. Waking up was the only option.

PLACES to HIDE

They released two tigers down at the end of 32nd Street, where all the new apartments are. It wasn't hard for the tigers to adapt. There was plenty to eat. Places to hide. In a year there were six more of them.

A TAXI SONG

His mom used to be a taxi driver and actually wrote lyrics that someone made into a song. Every time I visited, she said she would let us know when it played on the radio. Once she told me I just missed it. While we were in the basement, she would lurk by the open door. She left it open so she would know where we were. A giant tank battle was in progress across the cement around the furnace. Many casualties. The kitchen radio was always playing.

where we were

someone in science fiction

THE SECOND TIME I MET LEE VAN CLEEF

He was my first boss in high school. I went to his house to do landscaping on the set of his spaghetti western. I became Clint Eastwood shoveling beauty bark all about the rhododendrons. I got tense and ready to draw every time he reappeared to check on my work. The second time he appeared in my life was in Reno Town, on a dead-end street at dawn. Even though the sun was up, no one else was around. I was pulled along like someone in science fiction when a voice called from a broken doorway. If I would just stay there, he'd be right back. He had the designs for a machine that could turn water into gasoline. I could have it, just wait, don't move. "It's all legitimate," he mumbled. It was only last week he made a deal with Lee Van Cleef.

A FACTORY on 32nd STREET

"A new report by The National Restaurant Association projects that industry sales will reach $1.2 trillion and the workforce will likely exceed 17 million by 2030."
 —*Pizza Magazine*, December 2019

The dark parking lot is full of cold and rain. Ovens steam the windows, smeared with the light of pinball machines and a TV football game. The door opens. Someone comes out carrying a flat cardboard box and gets into a car.

Elvis Poem #1

In the morning
she kicked the cat off her feet.
Her husband Leroy wasn't beside her
so she guessed it must be long past 5 AM.
He got up that early every morning
to work in the mines.

Elvis Poem #2

The sheets next to her were cold
when she finally opened her eyes.
She had a gold framed photo of Elvis
next to the clock. The hands pointed
9:07.

Elvis Poem #3

Memorizing her place inside their house
wasn't difficult, a matter of footsteps
to the bathroom and then out
to the kitchen and the TV.
She could have done it in the dark.

Elvis Poem #4

A photo of you
stuck with a magnet
to the iceberg refrigerator.

Elvis Poem #5

Nobody could tell her anything
she didn't already know about Elvis.
She set a pot of water on the burner
and unscrewed the instant coffee lid.
Her cat Aaron meowed for breakfast.

Elvis Poem #6

She made another orange juice pitcher
with three cups of cold water
and dipped her finger in to taste.
It sounded like a fire engine
somewhere far off in the distance
getting lost in circles.

Elvis Poem #7
There used to be things she needed
to stay busy during the day.
She learned some card tricks
but her husband hated magic.
There were things on the TV
she would watch every day.

Elvis Poem #8
So she turned on TV
and went to the couch where
she found herself sleeping awake.
She liked to dream herself
into the place of those TV people.

Elvis Poem #9
Sometimes she wished there was
something better than gameshows
to watch before the soaps came on.
"Who cares what the answer is?"
she asked her cat over in the sunshine
by the window watching birds.

Elvis Poem #10
She couldn't let him roam outside
she was afraid he might get hurt.
It was dangerous world.

Elvis Poem #11
Somehow hours could pass
when she was connected to TV
and there was nothing else to do.

Elvis Poem #12
A commercial reminded her
it was lunchtime. She imagined
her husband eating sandwiches
a mile underground. Sometimes
his coughing kept them awake at night.

Elvis Poem #13
"Good Lord, I almost forgot!"
The cat jumped and looked at her.
"Today's Friday!" The 12 o'clock news
reminded her. "Tonight we're going out!
I have to get my hair done. Imagine
forgetting that…"

Elvis Poem #14
It seemed like more than a week
waiting for Friday. Calendars kept it
at the edge of the page, where all the days
rushed and fell.

Elvis Poem #15
She turned the TV off and moved
to the window. "It's another hot one.
I sure am glad Leroy got the air conditioner
installed. I don't know how we survived
without it."

Elvis Poem #16
Her image in the mirror
brushed her hair
and looked through her.

Elvis Poem #17
The tar on the street was melting.
It was one of those summer days.
She fanned herself with a magazine
and wore sunglasses like a movie star.

Elvis Poem #18
She drove through town
listening to the radio.
Big signs of restaurants
and gas stations moved
on either side.

Elvis Poem #19
While her hair was put in curlers
she explained it all away.
"Well, I wish there was something
I could do about it, but I can't.
I've tried. You know all those
miracle diets you read about,"
she waved the magazine,
"You starve for a while
but it all comes right back!"

Elvis Poem #20
The silver hair dryer came down
over her head. She flipped pages
humming a song through the sound
of electricity.

Elvis Poem #21
She wore a plastic hairnet outside.
Tempted by a man selling ice cream
she told him, "No, I better not!
I'm saving my appetite for tonight.
My husband's taking me out for ribs.
But it sure does look good! Such a
perfect day for ice cream."

Elvis Poem #22

When she got home, her cat
came to the door from the bedroom
"Hello Aaron! What you been doing?
Sleeping, huh?" She removed the hairnet
and folded it to a small size. She took
Aaron in her arms, purring.

Elvis Poem #23

An hour later
she poured a bowl of milk
and got something for herself.

Elvis Poem #24

For a while the faucet dripped
making pools in her breakfast dishes.
The cat made a perfect circle
curled in the sunshine.

Elvis Poem #25
At 4 o'clock, she turned off the TV
and went to the bedroom. "Now, let's see…"
She opened the sliding door and leafed
through the colors of dresses, looking for
the right one that said Friday Night,
Ribs and Dancing!

Elvis Poem #26
She set up the ironing board
between the record speakers.
She tested the iron with a wet
fingertip, stretched the green
flower-print flat, looking for
creases and wrinkles while
"Love Me Tender" played.

Elvis Poem #27
When she played records
she thought of moments
and people she knew
and music made her remember.

Elvis Poem #28
She was going to vacuum
but the dust was only a day old.
She could do it tomorrow.

Elvis Poem #29
It was getting late.
Leroy should have been home.
"He better not be at the bar again!"

Elvis Poem #30
She could hear her neighbor's TV.
An Alka-Seltzer sing-along. She hummed
the tune like a nursery rhyme. A warm wind
blew to her from the open window.

Elvis Poem #31
Now he was an hour late.
She crossed her legs and set
the playing cards on the table.
"Where is he, Aaron?"

Elvis Poem #32
She imagined the worst things
she saw him digging through rocks
with his bare hands and shouting at black.
She was scaring herself, pacing the floor
in her best clothes.

Elvis Poem #33
The phone rang.
Suddenly she started to cry.

Elvis Poem #34
She picked up the phone
even though her voice was sawing
through her tears.

Elvis Poem #35
"You hear the news?"
Someone she knew was crying too.
"I can't believe it…"

Elvis Poem #36
She fell down a tunnel so deep
the words echoed after her
and it took a mile to catch up.

Elvis Poem #37
The voice on the phone said,
"They said it was an overdose."
Her arm bracing her was slipping.
"Carol…" she said, "What happened?"

Elvis Poem #38
"Elvis Presley passed away."

Elvis Poem #39
All the sadness of the world
came to her at once as she tried
to hang up the phone.

Elvis Poem #40
They used to have canaries in the mines
when there was death in the air
to see if people could survive.

Elvis Poem #41
Things happened like stars in constellations
that strung together made up her whole life.
When she was born, there was a bright star.
Another star appeared when she met Leroy.
There was a star for a 1959 car crash,
with a scar on her arm. She could see
every important moment of her life
like it was shining.

Elvis Poem #42
When she was a girl
records and photographs
Elvis Presley became a star.

TURNING to WATER

My grandfather set a long handled dipper in the crook of a young tree. In the summer you could see where the trunk had begun to grow over the metal and in a while it looked like the pan had been magically run right through the tree. I don't think it would ever occur to me to do that. In the winter that pot held a scoop of snow, turning to water when spring began.

ANOTHER WIN for SEABISCUIT

When we got back from the grocery, there
wasn't enough room in the fridge so I brought
a few items outside to the mailbox and put
them in there. A can of condensed milk.
Some eggs. A green pepper and an avocado.
I thought it was a pretty good solution.
Then at midnight I heard a clatter on the
road. I looked out the window and I could
see the big, dim shape of a racehorse beside
the opened mailbox. That old nag has been
terrorizing our neighborhood for years.

The ANTI-GRAVITY GRAVITY BELT

It's the only thing keeping me connected to the earth. If I wasn't wearing it, I'd be caught like a kite in a tree. Believe me, I know what I'm doing.

HERMAN SNOCK STEALS the SUN

Herman Snock caught the sun in a jar. In the morning when the sun was small and just hatching in the clouds, he leaned out his window and captured it. The sky turned black for days while the sun flapped against the glass trapped in his room. The world became frantic, owls flew in tired circles. People went to work all day in the dark. After a week, Herman brought it to school with him. The sun was in a paper bag, making orange light for him to see. There were stars in the sky. The moon's creaking noise went over and over the city. He ran towards a friend in the schoolyard. "I've got the sun!" he yelled and held up the lantern color. Then to prove it, he opened the bag. The sun had been waiting all that time for a chance.

The BUFFALO ROAD

A road outside of town had a field with buffalo. I think there were three. The sight of them always took me by surprise. To think there was a time when they covered this land. I'd like to check on them today but I have no idea where that road was, it's not a way I go anymore.

The USED BELUGA

The aquarium was going out of business, each window had a price tag label. A lot of animals were already sold. I thought about getting a seal but I was too late. People were running from tank to tank. I was lucky to find a starfish at a reasonable cost.

The FAMOUS LAST WORDS of a DINOSAUR TRAINER

"A rolled up newspaper swatted on the end of the nose will let it know when it's done something wrong."

HEDDA HOPPER

This morning I rode a talking bus. When did they start talking? A mechanical woman's voice called out street names like a Hedda Hopper newsreel giving directions to the Homes of the Hollywood Stars, stopping only long enough to breathe on a cigarette.

MY NEW FOLLY

As often as I can, I watch a 1966 black and white Japanese television show. There are no subtitles. I have only the barest understanding of what's happening. A gondola gets attacked by a giant ape. It staggers through miniatures like a sleepwalker. What exactly happened in the end? Was it poisoned? Do apes really drink milk from the bed of a truck? Why has it fallen asleep in the middle of a city, with its back against a building?

MOVIE IDEA

Perfect movie to be filming in today's weather: **The Bellingham Divers Association.** Two divers (man and woman) in diving gear (flippers, suits, tanks, masks, snorkels) carrying between them a child also dressed as diver. The kid is pretending to swim while held in the air, looking around, examining the leaves of a rhododendron, picking up a wet pinecone.

A HYMN to RAKING LEAVES

He appeared in a field full of trees and stared at the covered ground. After he spent an hour raking leaves for the minister, he wondered if this was purgatory. Each day he would clear the yard, then the next morning he would get up and do it again. For the moment, that's why he was here. She was a friend of the family and offered him a room to stay in while he looked for one of his own...and for another job in town. Faith meant everything. Here he was, in a new place, starting all over from scratch.

CONFESSIONS of an INVENTOR

I've always wanted to be an inventor. There's good money in it. If you can come up with a good idea. That's the trouble, I can't. Not yet. I keep waiting for something. Who knows when that will happen?

The MAN WHO MARRIED a DREAM

"Can you be in my dreams every night?" he asked her and she promised she would. Each day he was just getting through so he could go to sleep and be with her. Morning was another world he didn't want to see.

the girl on the magic trapeze

A FIELD in OREGON

It might have been a farm for a while,
cleared from an even older age of dark forest,
long before there were words like field or
Oldsmobile. Now it was somewhere to pull
in the car, with a big wave of blackberry vines
to park behind and we were hidden from
the road. My cousin and I wanted to sleep
under the stars like we did when we were
kids. Who knows, we could have stayed there
until the field turned into something else,
leaving memory like bones. For now, it was
somewhere to unroll sleeping bags, the start
of a series of adventures, roads that turn into
other roads and tar that flows by the mile all
across America.

HERE in MISSISSIPPI

It's 10:33 in the morning. The flowers are watered. Cars on the highway make a constant sound. Won't it be wonderful when the gas runs out and we return to a beautiful world?

The WITCH'S HOUSE

Walking in the woods, there are no more bird songs. In quiet, I find a house sparkling with sugar coating. Everything on it is made of candy. What am I supposed to do? Ignore it?

15

Not many people believe in them, let alone have one in their possession and then decide to let it go. The porch door opened and a girl stood there in pale sunlight. She looked across the yard, the fallen hand-sized yellow leaves, towards the woods that grew thick behind the house. For fifteen years she kept a unicorn in her room.

all that water

WASHED ASHORE

It really got raining hard about 30 miles from home. The traffic on the highway slowed to 45, the road was slick and every car threw a spray in their wake. When we got home, the driveway was a shallow river. The gutters overflowed and all that water splashed as we hurried through the downpour into the house. We turned the lights on, got the heat going, and when I looked past the window curtain, I saw the submarine in our front yard. All the bolts and plates shined with the light from our house. Its propeller spun like a flower trying to get it back to the sea.

TRIBUTE to RED SKELTON

How did I end up in a gallery full of clown portraits, talking about composition, color, the expressive qualities of a painted face? It was my own doing. After years of walking past the store on Queen Anne hill, I finally went in. Red Skelton had recently died and I told the lady at the counter I was sorry to hear the news. She wouldn't let me leave until I went all round the room with a compliment for every clown on the wall.

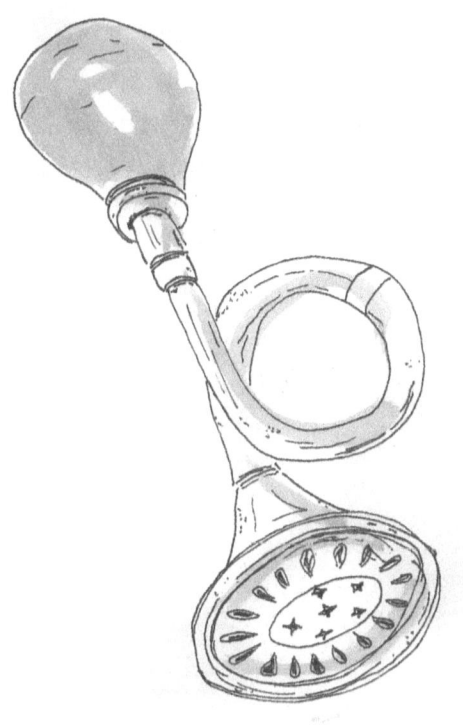

sorry to hear

WEARING a 1944 MOVIE

In black cloak and fedora, she wraps a
veil across her face and says, "Take me to
Martinique." Hide aboard this fishing boat,
she is told. Step on but don't fall out, the
ocean is rough and dark tonight. If we run
into trouble, expect a hail of bullets. I don't
want to lose you, I need the reward. Keep
your eyes upon the sea, watch the compass
glowing green. The world didn't invent being
afraid or send us around like shadows, we did
it to ourselves.

The COMEDIAN

Of course we went to see him when he came to town. We even walked by the theater earlier in the day and looked at his tour bus in hopes that he might by chance walk outside with a flowerpot. That night we were sent to the balcony to find our seats, all the way in back, under the projection booth. When the curtains opened, he came out on stage and we laughed. He was small as the wick of a candle.

SOMETHING to REMEMBER the FOREST BY

The dog and I had come to the end of the wooded trail, just before the parking lot started, and that's where someone had set up a souvenir shop. It wasn't much more than a bus stop. A table was piled with autumn leaves, branches, pine cones, stones from the creek. I picked up a soft owl feather and set it down. I listened to the field recording of wind in the trees.

The CATTLE BARON

Now I have two Guernsey cows in our front yard. The parched lawn has been gnawed, trampled and pockmarked by their hooves. The flower garden I was so proud of, forget about it. That's history. I don't know what I was thinking. They get bigger every day. My van makes endless trips filling up with hay. They stand beside the fence and watch the cars go by. Every half hour the bus growls past and nearly causes a stampede. Time after time I have to round them up into some semblance of calm. You think that's easy? It's tiring waking up at dawn, putting on my ten gallon hat for the routine of daily chores. There seemed to be only one end. Last night I left the gate open. As I fell asleep I thought that's it, my troubles are over and in my dreams I was actually free. Then it occurred to me— what my next herd should be—something simple and kept in a gilded cage. Canaries.

WATCHING ESTHER WILLIAMS with MY DAUGHTER

She lives in a fish tank. You may see her walking around everyday sights, working in an office, dining at the Casa Cugat club, dancing or driving a convertible, but sooner or later a mermaid always returns to the water. Her time below the waves is different than the life above, she has talents all her own, and we can only stay in the air and watch.

DANTE'S GRILL

Yes, I did work at Dante's back in those days when you had to get a job with just enough money to pay rent for a room in a basement and a little extra left over. A teenager showed me the way to cook a basket full of fries, boiled in oil, with burgers sizzling lined on the grill. Dante wrote about levels, a map of his descent into hell. This one wasn't all bad. I lasted a few weeks until I found a café that was better, a step up, or so I thought.

FAY WRAY ISLAND

Afterwards she would visit the zoo where King Kong was all bandaged up. He sat on the concrete and ignored the kids with their biplane toys, buzzing and laughing at him. No, he wasn't so ferocious anymore. The keeper let her stand on his shoulder with a spoon as big as a shovel. The medicine and rest would make him better. The thought of her was always large as a movie in his mind. When he closed his eyes, he was small enough to be held gently in her hand as she sung him to sleep and left him on that fog bound island where he belonged.

The WITCH'S DOG

Neither one of them could touch water. It burned their skin. "I'm sorry," she told her dog. "You'll have to stay indoors." So the dog stood by the window and watched that gray sky and waited all day for it to dry.

The MAGIC SHOP

The rabbits are on strike. They're lined up on the counter in a white row, carrying signs and shaking their fists in the air. Back and forth between the register and the crystal ball, if their demands aren't met they will never hide in a top hat again. The American Society of Magicians is taking the matter seriously but behind closed doors they are secretly negotiating with chinchillas.

JESSE JAMES & RIMBAUD

He wore a disguise into the post office. His WANTED poster watched from the wall. He hoped his other face looked like someone else. He waited in line and held his hand near his eyes. Being an outlaw meant being nobody. The window was open. The spring rush of the Missouri River roared like a steam engine on the run. Why take chances going into town? Why would he send a French poet a string of haiku that could be unfurled in Abyssinia, set free to find rooftops to sing from?

10 FEET off the GROUND

I was in a rush and I overinflated the puppy. She sailed off her paws and floated to the end of her leash, ten feet off the ground. There wasn't much to do but wait for her to come back down. In the meantime I took her to the park like I planned to. No sense wasting a sunny day. Careful, easy does it, I had to guide her between the branches above the path. She kicked her legs trying to catch a moth. Just like flying a kite, I had to pull on that line to keep her from getting tangled in a tree.

WITHOUT HAMLET

He never made it to the theater. One obstacle after another stopped him from getting there. So the play went on without their star. The cast adapted to their lives without him. Any mention of him gradually disappeared until he was forgotten. Ophelia took a job at a laundromat. The sound of washing machines surround her.

The WILDLIFE on 32nd STREET

Two houses away from us, lives a deer and a bighorn sheep. Sometimes I'll catch sight of them if the curtains are open. Their heads look down from the wall. They go about their days and nights without moving. Maybe music plays softly from their antler antennas.

PRINCE CHARLES

Not sure where he's going under a backpack
in the woods with the night coming on.
Will he sleep in the cradle of a tree? Dark
as a blackberry. Sour apples spoiling on the
ground.

LONZO

Everyone knew that chasing cars would be the end of that bulldog, but he never learned. He would hear the motor and the rubber tread and run at the street until he hit that passing blur, catching as much as he could in his teeth. Finally it happened, bit to a whitewall, taken round whirling three or four times until the car stopped and he was flat enough to fold.

WATCHING the WHALES

Drive the sailor a thousand miles from the sea, drop him on a lonely chair, but the ocean goes with him. In a goldfish bowl. Beside it is a telephone wired to a sunken ship. He can hear the mermaids singing each to each. He likes to watch them swim. Instead of goldfish, he thinks of them as whales.

The MUSEUM of FLUID MEMORY

Stop on the incline of a wooden bridge and look at the water. The glass is textured just so to resemble the rumple of a swollen stream. The canopy of berries and leaves is painted. No detail is left undone, even the trail of a water strider is included. Below the surface, a fish in the shadows looks real enough to slide past your eyes.

The DRAGONFLY JUNKYARD

A weedy lot stacked with the remains of old dragonflies. Broken wings are leaned against the fence like rows of stain glass windows. Motors with the gears pulled out. The long rusted segments of fuselage. The man who works here says to look around, there are enough parts about to mix and match and put another dragonfly in the air.

The SWEEPER

He didn't stop with the leaves. He swept every bit of grit and leaned into the broom to clear the cement. When it was dust, below that was earth and he kept going. Who knows how much history is swept aside with that broom? The cloud made it hard to see, but I'm guessing he's down there now with the dinosaurs.

The CAVEMAN

I was watching the cul-de-sac, the spot where the path to the woods began. It's winter, all the trees looking like scratches and out of their shadows walked a caveman. He was just the way you would expect—wearing fur skins and carrying a club. He got closer. Staring out the window at him might be a bad idea.

IT HELPS to KNOW SOMEONE

He was the butcher at Food Giant. When his daughter was looking for a job he got her hired as a checker. She was right out of high school and didn't know what to do with the rest of her life. He worked along the back wall of the grocery store and she would pass by and wave on her way to the breakroom. For 25 years.

HAUNTING the HOUSE

The town had a haunted house. It was on the registry and protected. Nevertheless, the ghost who lived there still had to pay rent and utilities. What good is a haunted house without mysterious lights glowing in the middle of the night? So the ghost got a part-time job at the grocery store, stocking shelves and sweeping aisles and haunting the house when it got home

VINCENT PRICE and the FLORIST

That must have been 1982. The year she spent in Hollywood. She didn't hear the door open, he was just suddenly before her, holding orchids. Sunglasses hid his eyes.

1982

reliable witnesses

In DEFENSE of MOTHRA

What's the wingspan of that beast? Nobody knows. There are no reliable witnesses. Look what happened to Osaka. There's not much defense against the storm it creates. What can we do? How did we get ourselves into this mess? A giant moth has pinned down Japan.

The FIVE & DIME ROBOT

I thought a lot about it. I imagined it in my room, walking across the carpet, buzzing and sparking and swinging its tin arms. The key on its back would spin until it ran down. It could knock over wooden blocks and the railroad track. After a while it would have a change of heart and repair the ruins it left behind. I could turn the key and it would pull a paper boat full of plastic animals.

UNDER YOUR SPELL

This dream was ending quickly, we could
all tell, so we were lined up waiting to leave.
The paint was peeling off the old walls. She
was just ahead of me and I followed her
out the door. "Another day at the factory," I
said. Tired of making cobblestones, chaining
together scenery, something monotonous for
the background. She surprised me by taking
my hand and giving it a squeeze. I remember
her eyes and the funny look she gave. The
parking lot was sunny, morning had arrived.

The LAST TELEGRAM

You paid by the word so you made a few
simple sentences look like a poem. It would
be sent over the wire and someone far
away would hear a knock on their door.
A uniformed messenger would deliver the
telegram. It didn't seem so miraculous then,
those everyday messages shared the air with
the passenger pigeons.

VIOLET of the SILENT MOVIES
July 27, 2019-Winter 2020
Elvis 42: Watering Garden Books, 1989.

asleep on the earth

Page from *The Robotic Age* (2018)
Illustrated by Aaron Gunderson

Books by Good Deed Rain

Saint Lemonade, Allen Frost, 2014. Two novels illustrated by the author in the manner of the old Big Little Books.

Playground, Allen Frost, 2014. Poems collected from seven years of chapbooks.

Roosevelt, Allen Frost, 2015. A Pacific Northwest novel set in July, 1942, when a boy and a girl search for a missing elephant. Illustrated throughout by Fred Sodt.

5 Novels, Allen Frost, 2015. Novels written over five years, featuring circus giants, clockwork animals, detectives and time travelers.

The Sylvan Moore Show, Allen Frost, 2015. A short story omnibus of 193 stories written over 30 years.

Town in a Cloud, Allen Frost, 2015. A three part book of poetry, written during the Bellingham rainy seasons of fall, winter, and spring.

A Flutter of Birds Passing Through Heaven: A Tribute to Robert Sund. 2016. Edited by Allen Frost and Paul Piper. The story of a legendary Ish River poet & artist.

At the Edge of America, Allen Frost, 2016. Two novels in one book blend time travel in a mythical poetic America.

Lake Erie Submarine, Allen Frost, 2016. A two week vacation in Ohio inspired these poems, illustrated by the author.

and Light, Paul Piper, 2016. Poetry written over three years. Illustrated with watercolors by Penny Piper.

The Book of Ticks, Allen Frost, 2017. A giant collection of 8 mysterious adventures featuring Phil Ticks. Illustrated throughout by Aaron Gunderson.

I Can Only Imagine, Allen Frost, 2017. Five adventures of love and heartbreak dreamed in an imaginary world. Cover & color illustrations by Annabelle Barrett.

The Orphanage of Abandoned Teenagers, Allen Frost, 2017. A fictional guide for teens and their parents. Illustrated by the author.

In the Valley of Mystic Light: An Oral History of the Skagit Valley Arts Scene, 2017. Edited by Claire Swedberg & Rita Hupy.

Different Planet, Allen Frost, 2017. Four science fiction adventures: reincarnation, robots, talking animals, outer space and clones. Cover & illustrations by Laura Vasyutynska.

Go with the Flow: A Tribute to Clyde Sanborn. 2018. Edited by Allen Frost. The life and art of a timeless river poet.

Homeless Sutra, Allen Frost, 2018. Four stories: Sylvan Moore, a flying monk, a water salesman, and a guardian rabbit.

The Lake Walker, Allen Frost 2018. A little novel set in black and white like one of those old European movies about death and life.

A Hundred Dreams Ago, Allen Frost, 2018. A winter book of poetry and prose. Illustrated by Aaron Gunderson.

Almost Animals, Allen Frost, 2018. A collection of linked stories, thinking about what makes us animals.

The Robotic Age, Allen Frost, 2018. A vaudeville magician and his faithful robot track down ghosts. Illustrated throughout by Aaron Gunderson.

Kennedy, Allen Frost, 2018. This sequel to *Roosevelt* is a coming-of-age fable set during two weeks in 1962 in a mythical Kennedyland. Illustrated throughout by Fred Sodt.

Fable, Allen Frost, 2018. There's something going on in this country and I can best relate it in fable: the parable of the rabbits, a bedtime story, and the diary of our trip to Ohio.

Elbows & Knees: Essays & Plays, Allen Frost, 2018. A thrilling collection of writing about some of my favorite subjects, from B-movies to Brautigan.

The Last Paper Stars, Allen Frost 2019. A trip back in time to the 20 year old mind of Frankenstein, and two other worlds of the future.

Walt Amherst is Awake, Allen Frost, 2019. The dreamlife of an office worker. Illustrated throughout by Aaron Gunderson.

When You Smile You Let in Light, Allen Frost, 2019. An atomic love story written by a 23 year old.

Pinocchio in America, Allen Frost, 2019. After 82 years buried underground, Pinocchio returns to life behind a car repair shop in America.

Taking Her Sides on Immortality, Robert Huff, 2019. The long awaited poetry collection from a local, nationally renowned master of words.

Florida, Allen Frost, 2019. Three days in Florida turned into a book of sunshine inspired stories.

Blue Anthem Wailing, Allen Frost, 2019. My first novel written in college is an apocalyptic, Old Testament race through American shadows while Amelia Earhart flies overhead.

The Welfare Office, Allen Frost, 2019. The animals go in and out of the office, leaving these stories as footprints.

Island Air, Allen Frost, 2019. A detective novel featuring haiku, a lost library book and streetsongs.

Imaginary Someone, Allen Frost, 2020. A fictional memoir featuring 45 years of inspirations and obstacles in the life of a writer.

Violet of the Silent Movies, Allen Frost, 2020. A collection of starry-eyed short story poems, illustrated by the author.

Next from Good Deed Rain...

From the top of the tree, I can see all Seattle, the buildings and clouds and Olympic Mountains to the west and on a clear day Mount Rainier. Closer by, I see the church spire and our green house and my bedroom window below the eaves. This is how the birds feel, this is why they sing. I sit up there and listen to the neighborhood. Other kids playing, a dog barking, a radio, a crow, a car on Woodlawn Avenue, my name called from the ground.

Raining

www.ingramcontent.com/pod-product-compliance
Lightning Source LLC
Chambersburg PA
CBHW031122080526
44587CB00011B/1081